SASSONA NORTON

SASSONA NORTON

FOREWORD BY STEVEN MILLER

ESSAYS BY ANN LANDI & HILARIE SHEETS

MORRIS MUSEUM

MORRISTOWN, NJ

To Reed, whose love has nurtured my creative voice.

CONTENTS

FOREWORD *Reflections on My Talks with Sassona Norton* by Steven Miller

Wᴴᴇɴ ɪ ꜰɪʀsᴛ sᴀᴡ ᴛʜᴇ sᴄᴜʟᴘᴛᴜʀᴇs of Sassona Norton, I was struck by how forthright they are. The sculptures are neither shy nor demure. Although they have a poetic side, they are quite strong. The same might be said about the artist.

Experience has taught me to be wary of artists' talk about messages in their work. Most artists prefer to let the work speak for itself. Often, the more they talk the weaker the work becomes. This is not the case with Sassona. Far from it. In fact, I have found my conversations with her to be quite revealing. While every piece holds its own alone—as should always be the case— Sassona's comments are always instructive. Without any introduction her work is engaging. But the artist's commentary can make it more complex and self-revealing.

In looking at Sassona's sculptures it is clear that she has a strong personal way of viewing life, and her figures are her ideal expressive vehicle. The work is about human emotions: feelings, thoughts, yearnings, desires, and insights. Sassona has deliberately chosen the human body as the simplest and most obvious forum for three-dimensional discussions with herself. Upon the conclusion of a piece, her particular internal conversations are exposed, literally and figuratively (pun intended), for all to respond.

Sassona deviates from the tradition to which she is connected by the choices she makes in both concept and execution. For starters she rejects the traditional singular emphasis on beauty or a narrow formulaic perspective. In spite of the evidence of remarkable knowledge in anatomy, the work is neither cosmetically pretty nor anatomically academic. These are storytelling works of art rooted in a special and personal truth that offers a more complex psychological narrative than the one expressed in previous centuries. The work is very well connected to the twentieth/twenty-first-century experience of living with uncertainty and ambiguity.

As Sassona often says, she is interested in expressing the coexistence of solitude and reaching out, strength and vulnerability, loss and longing, and the experience of time passing. I am particularly struck by the aspects of longing and time, and the connection between the two. Bronze is heavy, solid, static, and unchangeable. To express the dynamics of time Sassona sculpts her figures caught in the midst of a movement. Even when they stand still they seem to "jump off" in a very delicate balance between being anchored here and moving elsewhere. "I am interested in the dialogue between reality and wishes," Sassona said in one of our many talks, "and I like the challenge to express a constant process in material that does not move." That statement led us to a discussion about longing, the other aspect that attracts attention.

Longing, it turns out, is a main emotional component in Sassona's sculptures. Although she often talks about the "fundamental human condition," and strips her sculpture from any attribute that will anchor it in a specific time, she gives voice to one of the most prevalent characteristics of the individual condition in our era, namely loneliness. But when she combines it with expressions of longing, an unexpected sense of hope emerges. A bit unconventionally, Sassona does not think about longing in melancholy terms. "Longing,"

she said, "is the propelling power behind change. If you are dissatisfied with the reality of your life—without longing, you will have no desire to alter it. You might as well lie down, shrivel, and die."

In speaking of the nude as her chosen subject, Sassona says her pieces are naked rather than nude, an interesting differentiation that expresses vulnerability and exposure rather than a more idealized naturalism. Yet to my eye they are hardly overtly naked. They lack the feeling of being unclothed. Their sensuality is not suggestive. Perhaps it has to do with the absence of distracting anatomical detail and the artist's emphasis on wonderfully articulated surfaces and a certain patina. More likely it has to do with the overall force of each piece and the expressions it emanates.

Adding to the nude/naked conundrum is the fact that Sassona's figures are bald. I asked her about this very obvious choice. She said: "If they had hair, what style hair would it be?" Good point. As we see in movies, hairstyles, especially for women, immediately document the time when the movie was made. This tends to happen with sculpture too, unless it is attempting to be "timeless." Sassona also noted that the baldness gives her figures greater vulnerability.

Our conversation about nudity, nakedness, baldness, and styles helped explain to me why Sassona chooses to sculpt mostly women. "It is not because I am one," she says. "Men's baldness would not have made the same statement as women's in terms of vulnerability. I am interested in creating the drama of contradictions between that and strength. While the woman's reaching out spells yearning, the muscularity of her body expresses power. The latter was atypical of women in the past. Consequently it connects it to a social and personal achievement of our time. I could not accomplish this particular dialogue by sculpting a man."

Contrary to many sculptors who work in the figurative tradition, Sassona rarely uses a model. She envisions the pose and might engage a model for a few hours to determine the logistics of movements. "I use the model," she says, "only as a visual dictionary for some anatomical details that change when a certain movement takes place." No resemblance to the actual model will ever be present in the finished work.

Another unusual feature involves Sassona's decision to start sculpting in the full size of the finished work. Most sculptors make drawings or build maquettes first. Sassona does not engage in any such preparatory processes. "A lot of the final modeling and shaping is spontaneous and organic," she says. "I can create it only by working with my hands, without any tools. It means that I need a large surface to work on which cannot be pre-created in a smaller size." She smiles when I tell her that this is somewhat precarious: her work must be envisioned entirely in her mind ahead of time, not an easy task based on the large scale that she uses. "This adds to the excitement of the discovery," she says.

Scale is a very important element of Sassona's work. All her sculptures are larger than life. The figures are over life-size, she explained in one discussion, for the same reason they are muscular: to express strength. The calculation of the scale is deliberate. While the figures are larger than life, they are not overwhelmingly so. It is crucial to retain a level of approachability for the viewer. The work should have a sense of monumentality and drama without being unreachable.

Because of the tremendous weight of the clay, the sculptor cannot start sculpting without first creating a support system or armature. When Sassona and I discussed her process, it was immediately clear that her armatures had not only to be strong, but also capable of creating the gestures of the particular piece she was making. Indeed, in their simplicity, Sassona's armatures — large, heavy, and welded from steel bars—are quick line-drawings that capture the essence of where she wants to end up with a piece. "Clearly," she explained, "it is essential that the armature is mechanically well built and placed exactly at the center of each of the sculpture parts in order to support them properly. But there is another aspect. As naked as it is, the armature must stand on its own in artistic terms as if it were an independent piece. The movement must be expressed in its right proportions and dynamics. Otherwise the finished piece will be a failure."

While many sculptors terminate their involvement once a clay phase is finished, Sassona keeps sculpting after the sculpture is produced in wax, and spends long months working at Argos, the foundry she uses in Brewster, New York. "Very often," she explains, "what is acceptable in clay looks harsh in wax. The hardness of wax changes the quality of the texture. At times, I end up with such a different look that I may opt to create a new mold in order to preserve the changes."

Sassona pays close and careful attention to the bases her sculpture rests upon. For her large complete figures, the base is part of the work, often replicating the idea of a rock or other natural formation. Because the base is also cast bronze and has a similar patina to the sculpture, there is hardly any artistic separation

between the figure and what it is on. The base is part of an overall composition that both separates the sculpture from the world around it and connects it to that world.

In the case of Sassona's figure parts—legs and feet, hands, heads, etc.—she maintains a careful and precise division between the base and the piece. In some cases only a tiny part of the sculpture touches the surface of a base. This gives the piece its own space, independent of what holds it up.

At its essence, Sassona's sculpture is as much about temperament and emotion as it is about shapes, volumes, materials, voids, and weight. Her handwriting is evident on modulated surfaces that are as impressionistic as they are expressionistic. Her pieces are absolutely charged with individual personality. They are the story of both one person and many—a timeless, enduring achievement.

ESSAY *In the Hands of Sassona Norton* *by* Hilarie Sheets

IN THE HANDS OF SASSONA NORTON, the human form takes on deeply metaphoric dimensions. Her larger-than-life-size bronze sculptures—some full-length naked figures, others cropped heads, hands, or legs—all embody some kind of gesture of reaching. Muscular, torqued, dynamic, they yearn for something lost, they grasp for something more. This idea of longing, rooted in the pain of absence but fueled by the ambition and belief that the future holds promise, is an essential component of the human experience. The artist describes it as a duality between where you are and where you want to be, and it is the psychological underpinning of all her sculpture.

That Norton can capture such moments of transition and emotional ambiguity in a medium as immovable as bronze is another intriguing duality in her sculpture. In *Fleeting Light* (PLATE 7), for instance, a large-scale naked female figure with a powerful build and massive feet is anchored to a rocklike pedestal. Her upper body is thrown back almost violently with her arms outstretched and her face caught in an open-mouthed cry flickering between joy and sorrow. The movement of the figure seems dictated by the light of the window illuminating the entrance gallery where the sculpture is sited, and indeed Norton conceived of the piece with this interaction in mind. The sculpture is not only a virtuoso study of human form but it also personifies the feeling of desire and imminent loss in that last moment of beauty before the light fades.

The human figure has always been Norton's subject, even as a little girl growing up in Tel Aviv with an early propensity for drawing. She has a vivid memory of a time when she was five years old and figured out something fundamental about how to draw. She was drawing a girl in a dress with a stomach shown, but then she realized that when you look at a clothed person the stomach isn't actually visible, so she erased it. Norton calls it an "aha" moment of understanding that you have to draw what you see, not what you think is there.

Although her youth was dominated by making art, for which she was recognized by her teachers, that was not what she initially pursued professionally. Her father—a businessman she describes as a frustrated architect who always looked for opportunities to renovate buildings—and her mother wanted her to be a high-school teacher. She studied literature and theater at the Tel Aviv University, and pursued painting on her own time. While teaching high school in her early twenties she had a one-person show of her canvases that was highly praised in the local press. After several years of teaching she decided to shift into journalism, writing an art column in the largest Israeli daily newspaper while continuing to make art.

During this period she met an American art collector who ultimately asked her to come with him to the United States. She did in 1974, and they married and settled in New York City. Norton enrolled in the Art Students League and for the next five years spent eight hours a day working in the studio there as a

painter in what she characterizes as the most concentrated form of art education she'd ever had. Instructed by artists including Stanley Boxer, Bruce Dorfman, Marshall Glasier, and Leo Manso, from day one she was treated as a professional artist who was expected to produce serious work.

While the climate of the New York art world at that time favored abstraction—be it Minimalism, color field painting, or Abstract Expressionism—Norton bucked the trends and concentrated on the human figure, which for her felt like the most accessible vehicle for expressing her view of life and the world we live in. While many of her teachers were abstract artists, they never tried to push her in a different direction. The challenge for Norton during these years was finding her personal artistic vocabulary within an age-old figurative tradition.

Scale was something she began to play around with. Painting the figure larger than life was a way that Norton found to visually convey a sense of strength and weight that appealed to her. In her paintings, twisted outsized nudes, unmoored in the vacant space of the picture plane, push up against the edges of the canvases. At a certain point, instead of doing increasingly gigantic nudes, Norton chose to concentrate on a single element of the figure, predominantly hands, that she could blow up as big as she wanted.

Norton felt that hands are as expressive as a face but have a universal quality that faces do not have. They are anonymous, nameless, and therefore more abstract than faces while at the same time they offer a greater range of movements. Norton really began to find her voice in her series of paintings from the early 1980s—shown in solo exhibitions at Gallery 84 and Sutton Gallery in New York—that depict massive, faceted hands in a repertoire of clenched, emotional gestures.

The sculptural presence of these forms is palpable. It is tempting, with the hindsight of knowing Norton's trajectory as a sculptor, to look at the entities in these paintings as three-dimensional beings trying to break free of their two-dimensional constraints. Indeed, Norton recounts the repeated experience of running into people who were familiar with her paintings, yet would ask her how her sculpture was going. She would be taken aback and clarify that she was a painter not a sculptor, but today finds it interesting that people remembered the paintings as sculptures.

Then in the late 1980s Norton's husband became ill. He was sick for several years and Norton closed her studio and became his caregiver. He died in 1993 and for some time after, Norton was recouping from her devastating loss. As difficult as his death was for her personally, though, the hiatus in her working life opened a new window for her creatively. When the time was right for her to go back to art making, she knew it wouldn't be painting. As she describes it, the spell of comfort and inertia and familiarity had been broken and she could start fresh.

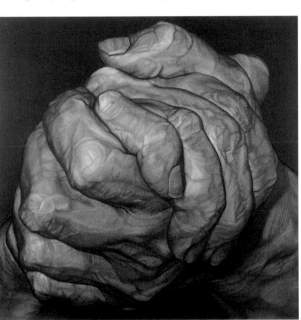

Supplication, 1995, Acrylic and Charcoal on Canvas, 50" × 50"

She found an instant affinity with a new medium the day she decided to walk in to a local art association near her home in New Jersey and take a three-day course on sculpting. It was the first time she had ever worked with clay and it felt completely natural for her. What's obvious to her now is that she had always seen the world in terms of shapes and weight—a kind of spatial way of thinking that she inherited from her father—rather than color, the language of painting. She immediately loved the directness and solidity of sculpting in clay with her hands. Norton then spent a month learning more about the sculpting process at the Sculpture Center in New York.

Since 1999, in a large garage she renovated into a studio, Norton has embraced the medium most suited to her temperament, producing an impressive and cohesive body of work in bronze. The first piece she completed is titled *Beyond Reach* (PLATE 1), a man's naked torso that echoes classical Greek and Roman marble fragments of the idealized male form. Yet Norton's figure has the realism of a much older man, sinewy and weathered. The surface of the bronze is heavily worked and abraded, yielding a tactile impression of human skin that stands in marked contrast to the hard, sleek areas where she has abruptly ended the sculpture—chopping it through the mouth and at the upper arms all lifted upwards. In open-ended terms, it speaks to the dichotomy between the physical and the spiritual, between isolation and aspiration.

From there, Norton reworked themes familiar from her paintings, such as hands, in three-dimensions. *Between Questions* (PLATE 3), for instance, is a single oversized hand that can stand upright on its wrist with thumb and forefinger raised as though interjecting a new point, or lie sideways in a kind of denouement. Creased, mottled, veined, it's a compelling object that tells different stories from different angles. In *To Whom Do I Pray* (PLATE 15), two gnarled, anguished hands, cupped in supplication, open upwards and metaphorically emit a silent cry. This piece was recently purchased by Henry Buhl, whose well-known collection of photography and sculpture focuses on the theme of hands and all their associative power.

In another piece, titled *Into the Wind* (PLATE 10), two meaty, calloused hands—pressed together at the wrists and palms—open their fingers outwards, like limbs of a tree being buffeted by the wind. There's a sense of both release and inability to hold on that shifts with changing vantage points. Turned and displayed on its side, one hand looks as though it has stumbled and is falling while the other tries to support it. In all these works, the hands seem almost stand-ins for fully realized figures.

This sense of the part speaking for the whole is particularly strong in the piece *I Thought I Was Dancing* (PLATE 13). Two stumps of lower legs knock together awkwardly with the toes of the oversized feet curling up bashfully. It reads as an abstraction of two figures in a first moment of intimacy, tentative and sweet, grop-

ing to get it right. Norton is clearly interested in how concentrating on segments of the body can deliver a powerful emotional punch. *The Edge of Rest* (PLATE 5) consists of two crossed lower legs braced by a hand, each abruptly severed mid-limb. It is ostensibly a position of repose, yet one foot is flexed in agitation, suggesting that a state of calm is hard to achieve or maintain. The tension of the piece is only exacerbated by the surreal termination of the limbs, with the slick ends patinated a hotter tone than the rest of the softly modeled bodily surfaces.

In a pair of works titled *Unquenchable Thirst* (PLATE 12) and *Memories of Sweetness* (PLATE 11), each has a huge disembodied head of a man hovering over a set of hands. In one, the face turns toward cupped hands for a drink; in the other, he reaches out for a kiss. The heads are attached to the hands at only a single point, requiring a special structural support. This lends them a floating quality that belies their considerable physical heft and adds to the sense of drama and surprise. Clearly the same man, the heads function as complements. As the titles indicate, the pairing embraces present and past, an active thirst for something that exists only in the realm of memories.

Norton's full-length figures, which are all naked women, are startling both in their monumentality and their conscious lack of prettiness. For one thing, she has chosen to portray them all bald, which has the effect of making them look more exposed and vulnerable while at the same time projecting strength. That, together with their disproportionately large hands and feet and rippling musculature, gives them formidable presence and a feminine-masculine duality that speaks to general human experiences. The baldness and lack of any other details that might have tied these figures to a certain period also help give the works their time-less and universal qualities.

Siting becomes important with these works. Rather than find a suitable place for a completed sculpture, Norton usually sculpts with a specific location in mind that dictates the conception of the piece. When she installs the sculptures outdoors, she often integrates them with fountains or pools of her own design. *First Rain* (PLATE 6), for instance, is a towering figure poised on a rock at the center of a circular fountain. Head bowed meditatively, arms outstretched, and palms raised, the figure appears to be conjuring the dance of the water with the gesture of her hands. For *The Last of Summer* (PLATE 8), Norton designed a reflecting pool in the shape of a cross. The huge female figure lying with legs bent at the center of the cross, a position inherently loaded with the idea of suffering, arches her upper body and reaches out dramatically with her oversized hands.

The unidealized realism of these figures brings to mind the work of the French sculptor Auguste Rodin (1840–1917), whose sculptures such as *The Burghers of Calais* (1884–1895) were groundbreaking in how they depict human anguish. As a teenager in Tel Aviv, Norton can remember the emotional impact of seeing a Rodin sculpture of a wizened older woman. She has found the tactility of his bronze surfaces and the exaggeration of certain features and gestures to be an important touch-stone. Her sculpture *One Last Word* (PLATE 4), of a woman sharply contorted in body and emotion as she looks behind her to say her final word, echoes the kind of postures of Rodin's *Burghers*, whose six fourteenth-century martyrs who sacrificed themselves for their city look back in fear rather than heroism.

The ambition in Norton's figures is impressive, both in their size and their complexity. *An Hour Before Dawn* (PLATE 2) has a Herculean-toned woman curled protectively over her legs. Yet she extends one open hand, indicating the tension between maintaining autonomy and accepting the potential for love. The tor-sion in the figure's pose is incredibly difficult to pull off technically—noteworthy because Norton is largely self-taught in the medium of sculpture.

Norton uses the lost-wax process to make her sculptures, a laborious method employed since antiq-uity that is still the best way to cast all the detail of modeled clay in bronze. For her, a piece starts as an image in her head. If it's going to be a full figure, she knows it will be big and emotional. Rather than do any preparatory studies—either drawings or small maque-ttes—she starts right off building a full-size armature in aluminum. Creatively, she responds best when working with the actual scale. Manipulating the pliable alu-minum is her method of drawing and the point where crucial decisions are made.

Once she has the armature—basically a giant stick figure that indicates the movements of the future sculp-ture—she has a welder copy it under her supervision in steel, which is strong enough to brace and support the weight of clay. She then fills out the steel armature with chicken wire and injects spray foam into the cavities that dries, fleshing out the figure. At this point, Norton pads the armature with clay and the real sculpting process begins. On a full figure, she might spend four to six months on the modeling. It is in this hands-on stage that Norton feels her mark is most directly imprinted on the material.

When she determines that the work in clay is complete, Norton has a mold made. Because of the large size and the complexity of extended limbs in most of her figures, the mold maker usually cannot do a single mold but rather makes numerous plaster molds of different sections. Then the molds go to the foundry and are cast in wax. Norton comes when the wax sections are poured and then starts to rework their surfaces using a heat gun and her hands.

Once the wax segments are complete, the foundry builds a gating system with pipes around each piece and dips it into a ceramic bath to create a ceramic shell. The pipes serve to support the wax and provide a drainage system for when the ceramic shell is put into the furnace at a very high temperature. The melted wax pours out—thus the "lost-wax"—and is replaced by molten bronze poured in. When the bronze has solidified, the ceramic shell is broken off. Once all the sections are welded back into a whole, Norton comes in again, and the surface of the bronze is mottled with a grinder to achieve the look of suppleness that is so important to her. She chooses the finished patina, but it takes layers of different acids applied to the work under torch to achieve the softness of the patina that she requires.

Surely Norton's most complex piece to date, one that required nine separate molds, is her Montgomery County 9/11 memorial that stands in the plaza of the county courthouse in Norristown, Pennsylvania, honoring those lost in the World Trade Center. For this, she adapted her theme of hands to enormous dimensions.

Two craggy, powerful hands—rising up over eight feet tall—cup a radically twisted and rusted section of an I-beam salvaged from the wreckage of the North Tower as though it were a bird ready to take flight.

Norton's participation in this memorial project began with the chance reading in *Sculpture* magazine of a call to the sculpting community asking for proposals for a 9/11 memorial. The county had retrieved the I-beam section through the FBI and the two stipulations of the project were that it incorporate the fragment and that it would be sited in the front of the county courthouse. Norton was in London at the time and couldn't visit the site, but immediately had the idea of two giant hands holding the I-beam and resting on a piece of polished black granite, low and horizontal. She wanted it both to have a reflective quality and to be monumental and intimate at the same time.

In early 2003 Norton sent in her proposal with drawings and text about her choices. She didn't hear anything for the next year. Then from out of the blue she received a notification that she was one of the six finalists out of the dozens of applicants from around the world that responded to the original call. Each of the finalists was given a stipend to cover the costs of building a maquette and appearing in front of the committee of judges. Norton next went to Norristown to see the courthouse and as she describes it her heart dropped because she knew her design wasn't going to work. The courthouse is a neoclassical building with huge fluted columns extending vertically from the ground floor to the roof. Nothing with a horizontal emphasis would make sense visually in front of this building and the plaza itself was smaller than she had anticipated.

Norton then did what she learned later no other finalist had done, which was to view the I-beam in person. What must have originally stretched 18 feet was folded in on itself three times, contorted and torn, with an organic quality that belied its industrial origins. Norton realized that the gravity line fell outside of the I-beam and that it made sense to angle this fragment and the hands on a tilt. Once she made that decision, others quickly fell into place. She needed something tall so she chose to support the hands on a square column. She needed to anchor the column so she decided to have it come off the periphery of a round disc. She proposed ringing the circumference of the disc with the inscription:

September 11, 2001. The many who died. The many who fought to save others. Memories never die.

Two weeks after her presentation to the judges, she was notified that she had won $100,000 to execute the memorial.

Four years after the tragedy of September 11, 2001, Norton's memorial, standing almost 18 feet high, was unveiled in the courthouse plaza of Norristown. In this powerful monument, Norton pushes her longtime exploration of hands—of their capacity to express ideas of endurance, love, support, aspiration—to another level that eloquently blends the private and public, the personal and the universal.

PLATES

PLATE 1 *Beyond Reach*, 2001, Bronze, 21" × 10" × 11"

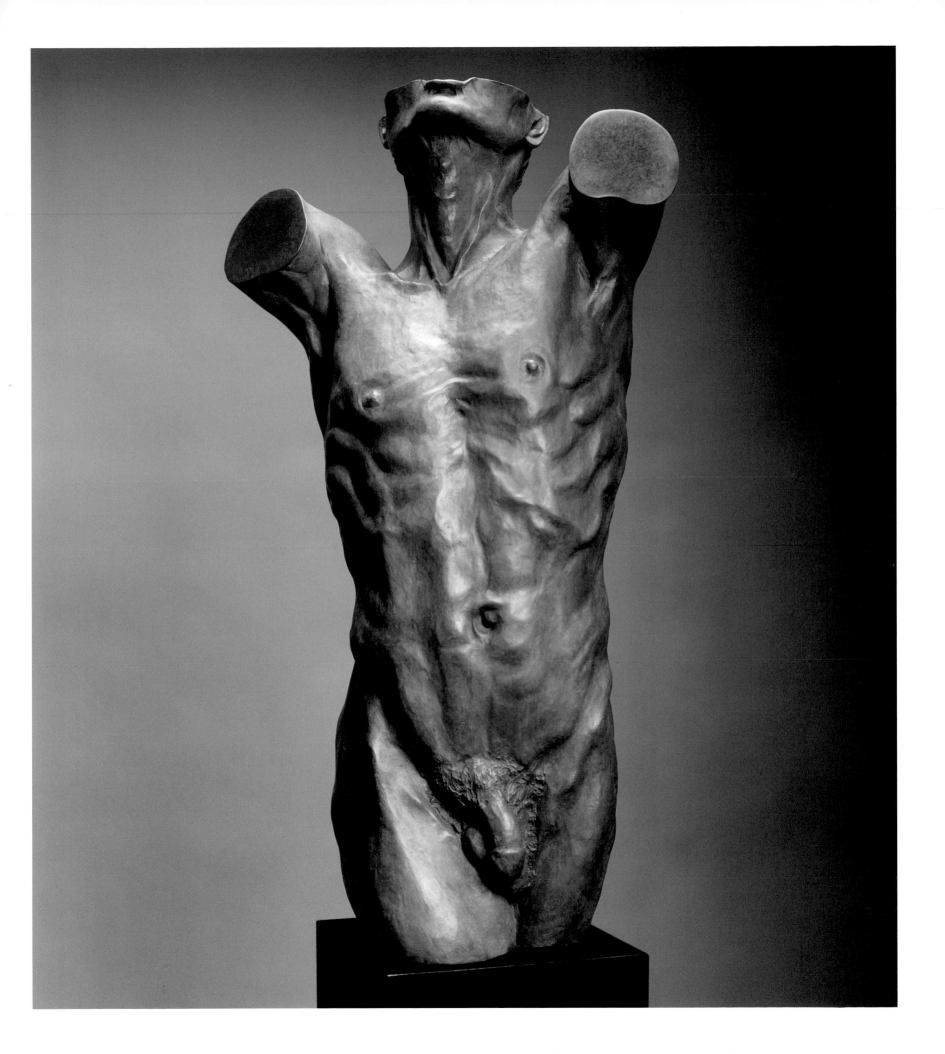

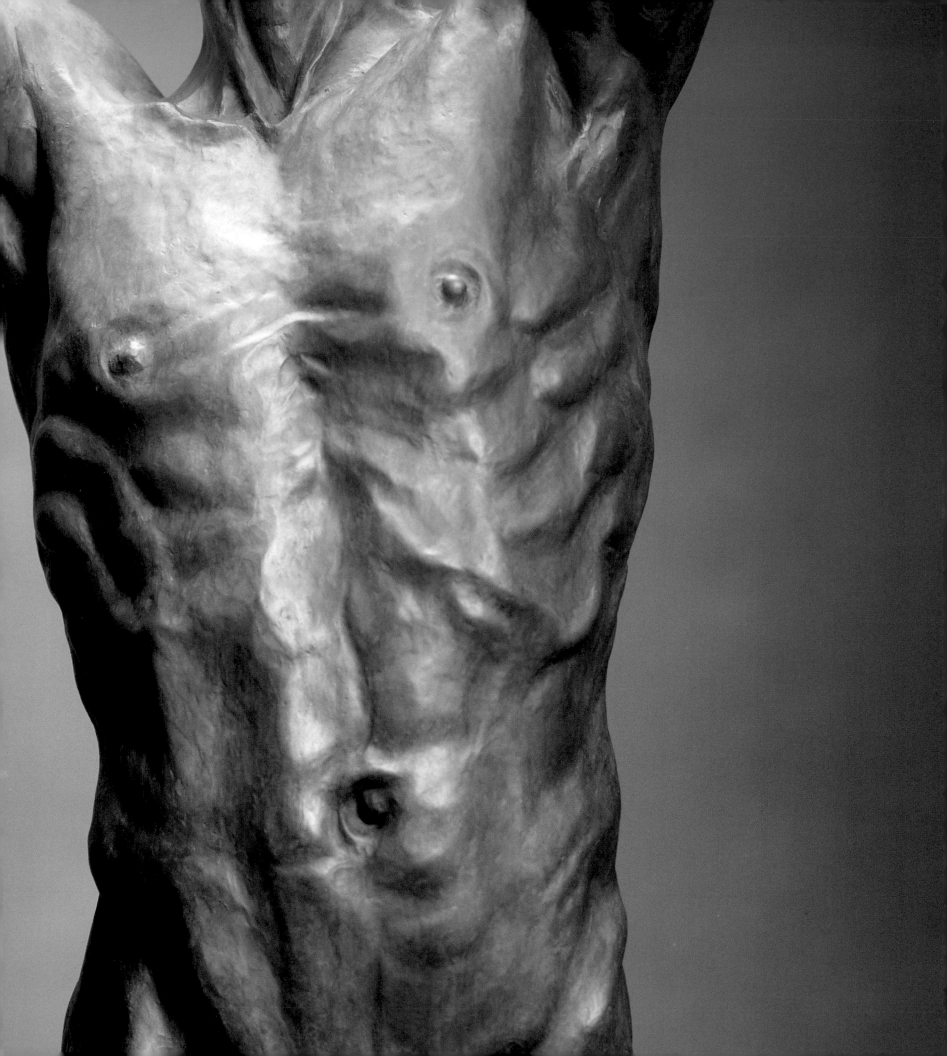

PLATE 2 *An Hour Before Dawn*, 2001, Bronze, 53 1/2" × 27" × 44"

PLATE 3 *Between Questions,* 2001, Bronze, $10^{1}/_{2}$" $\times$ $6^{1}/_{2}$" $\times$ $5^{1}/_{2}$"

PLATE 4 *One Last Word*, 2002, Bronze, 70" × 34" × 31"

PLATE 5   *The Edge of Rest,* 2002, Bronze, $10^{1}/_{2}$" × $12^{1}/_{2}$" × 18"

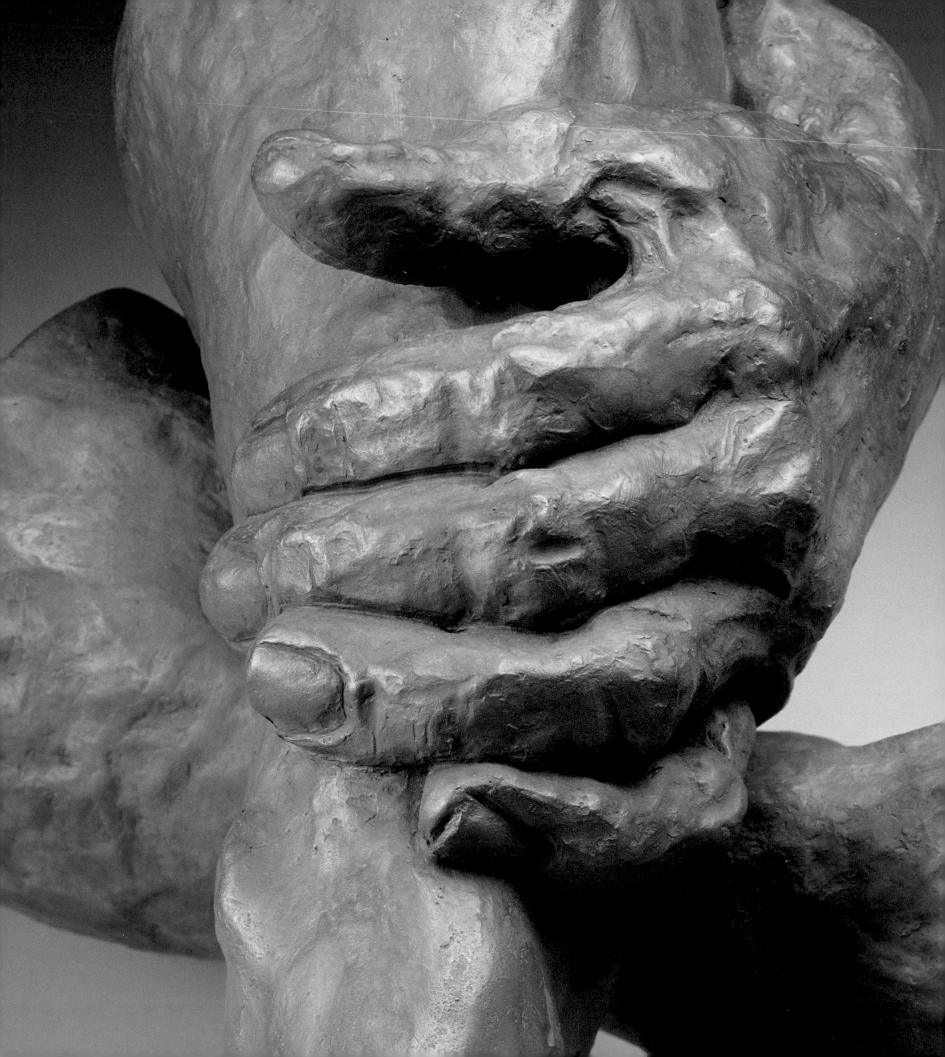

PLATE 6 *First Rain*, 2002, Bronze, 116" × 52" × 50"

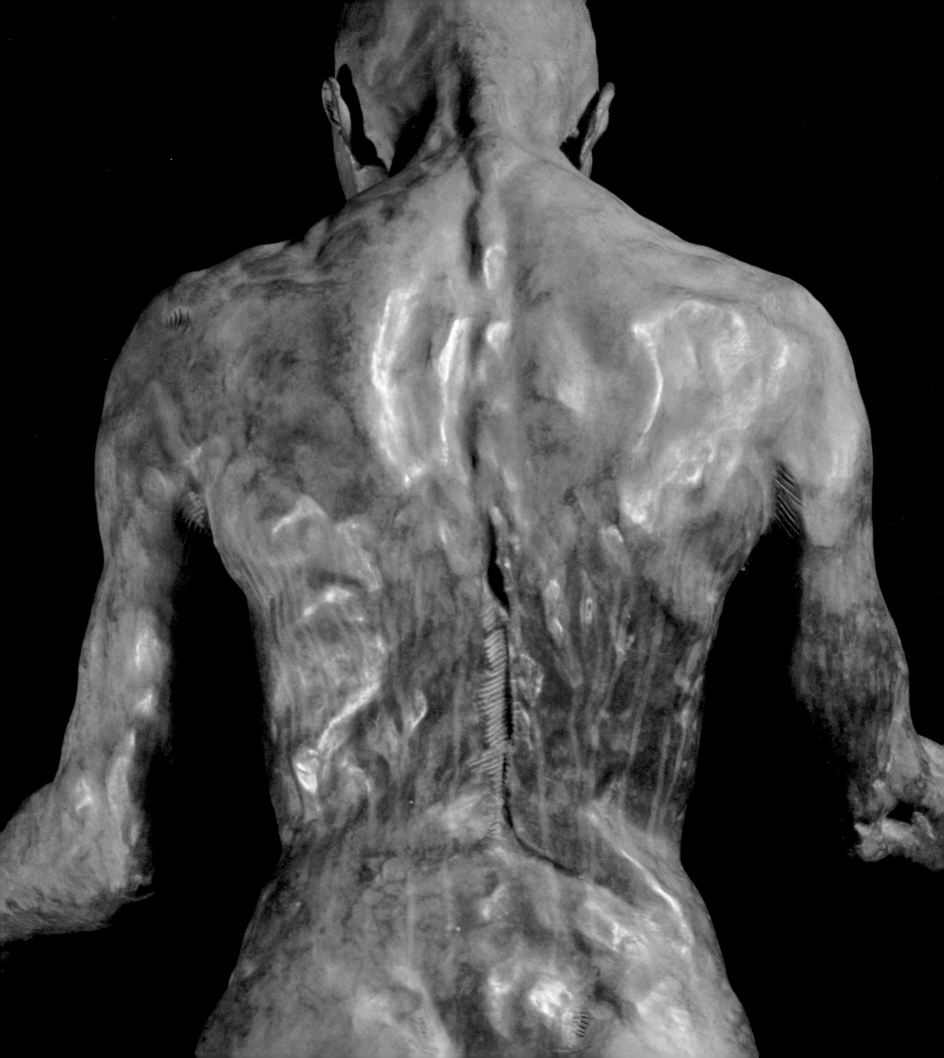

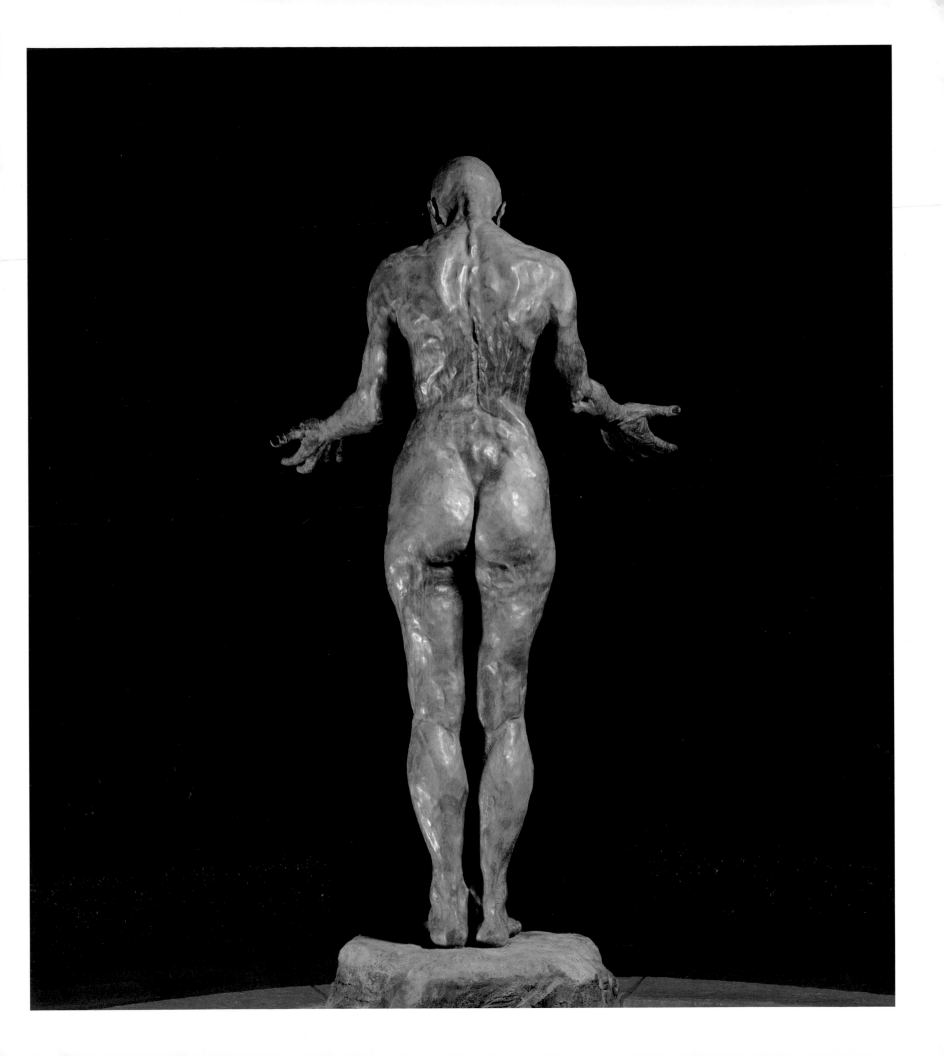

PLATE 7 *Fleeting Light,* 2003, Bronze, 100" × 66" × 71"

PLATE **8** *The Last of Summer,* 2003, Bronze, 53" × 96" × 86"

PLATE 9 *A Single Drop*, 2004, Bronze, $12^3/4$" $\times$ 11" $\times$ $7^3/4$"

PLATE 10 *Into the Wind*, 2004, Bronze, $16^{1}/_{2}$" $\times$ $20^{1}/_{2}$" $\times$ 11"

PLATE 11 *Memories of Sweetness*, 2004, Bronze, 26$^{1}/_{2}$" × 12$^{1}/_{2}$" × 17"

PLATE 12   *Unquenchable Thirst*, 2004, Bronze, 23$^{1}/_{2}$" × 11" × 15"

PLATE 13 *I Thought I Was Dancing*, 2005, Bronze, $34^1/_2$" × $20^1/_2$" × 17"

PLATE **14** *The Seed Cradle*, 2005, Bronze, $8^{1}/_{2}$" × 13" × $17^{1}/_{2}$"

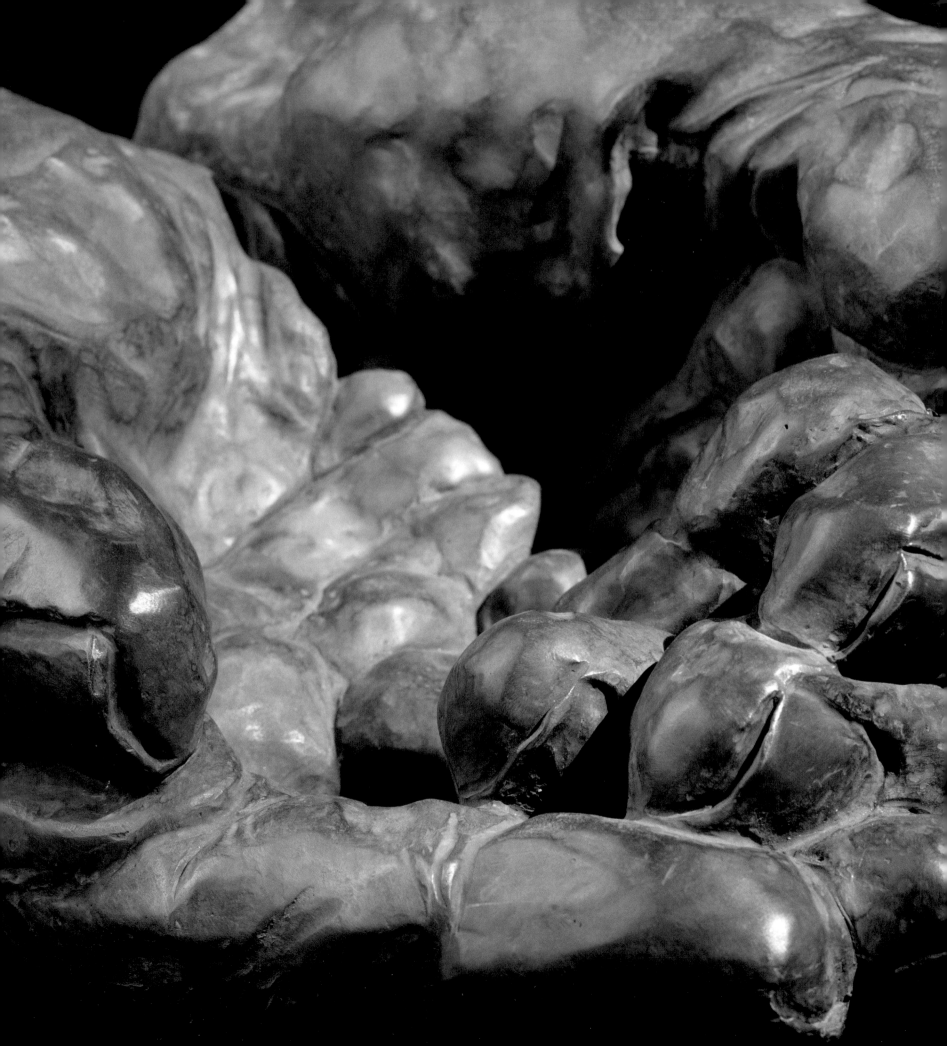

PLATE **15** *To Whom Do I Pray,* 2005, Bronze, 23^1/$_2$" × 18" × 15"

9/11 MEMORIAL

For THOUSANDS OF YEARS—ever since mankind was first able to chisel stone or push huge boulders into impressive formations—the desire to create monuments has been almost as elemental as the need to worship, build a community, or engage in warfare.

Different cultures looked to outsized, heroic sculpture to fulfill varying needs. The pharaohs and other rulers in ancient civilizations wanted enduring testaments to their power and stature, colossal statements that would elevate them to godlike dimensions (and perhaps remind the general populace of its inferior position in the grand scheme of things). The Greeks celebrated their pantheon, combining the human and the sacred in some of the most sublime and enduring works of art in all of Western civilization. With the Romans

and, later, the Renaissance came the notion of celebrating the individual in memorable public fashion: perhaps on a horse, as in the equestrian monuments of Marcus Aurelius or Donatello's likeness of Gattemalata, the great Venetian soldier, in Padua. Later public celebrations of individuals—one thinks of Houdon's marble statue of George Washington or Daniel Chester French's portrayal of Lincoln in Washington, D.C.—continue the tradition of paying special homage in stone or bronze to leaders whose accomplishments transcend the contributions of ordinary mortals.

But the notion of the monument as a memorial to specific events has a far less linear development in the history of art and is, in fact, a fairly recent phenomenon. The word "memorial" draws on the same roots as the word "memory." As such, a memorial offers and demands something different than a sculpture that is intended to celebrate the heroic individual. Such monuments, whether large or small, public or private, are meant to provoke reflection and remembrance.

There is a long and venerable history attached to grave markers and tomb sculptures meant to honor the dead. These embellish the sites where family and future generations can reflect on loss, transience, and perhaps the hope of resurrection in a future life. From the delicate reliefs on Greek grave stelae to Michelangelo's tomb sculptures for Giuliano de' Medici to scattered examples of more recent funerary monuments (and there are very few worth a second glance, one exception being Augustus Saint-Gaudens, late-nineteenth-century memorial to Clover Adams), these are works that invite contemplation of the nature of life and death and ask us to remember the person whose remains are laid to rest here.

These are all, however, testimonials to individuals. What of the memorial that bears witness to a larger and more terrible loss, to an event that took a huge toll in human lives? You will seldom find any kind of sculptural tribute to all the souls lost in the epic battles of history before the twentieth century. If Waterloo is to be remembered, it's in statues and paintings of the Duke of Wellington. Similarly, the triumphs and defeats of the American or French Revolution commemorate the heroes of those bloody wars or celebrate idealized individuals, as in François Rude's boisterous relief of La Marseillaise on the Arc de Triomphe in Paris. It's not until the late nineteenth century that the idea of paying tribute to ordinary mortals lost in the horrific

upheavals of history takes hold in the public and artistic imaginations. Augustus Saint-Gaudens' memorial to Robert Gould Shaw and his regiment, unveiled in Boston in 1897 and completed three years later, commemorates for the first time a group of real people who marched off in the service of their country and never came back. Borrowing the ancient prototypes of the sculptural frieze and the equestrian monument, Saint-Gaudens depicted the young colonel Robert Shaw leading his regiment of black soldiers, some of them former slaves, underneath a hovering figure of Nike, the goddess of Victory. But Shaw's men were not victorious. Three months after leaving Boston, in the summer of 1863, the colonel and most of his recruits were killed in a frontal attack in South Carolina and buried in a mass grave.

Saint-Gaudens' breathtaking memorial signaled something new in the history of art: the memorial not for an individual or for a brave leader, but for a group of people wiped out under devastating circumstances that were certainly not of their own devising. They were victims of history, and as history marched on into the next century, when the technologies for eradicating ever larger groups from the planet became ever more devastating, the need to remember those lost to warfare or other forms of global hatred has seemed especially acute. And so there are Holocaust memorials of many kinds for the millions murdered during the Nazi regime, and monuments for the soldiers, sailors, doctors, nurses, and others sacrificed during two world wars, as well as the conflicts in Korea and Vietnam. For the most part—the stunning exception being Maya Lin's Vietnam memorial in Washington, D.C.—these sites of remembrance have been figurative in approach. The reasons for that are many and varied. For one, the paradigm of the human figure is the one most easily grasped by the largest number of people; it doesn't take a "trained" eye to appreciate the statement being made. For another, figurative sculpture has a long and venerable history and connects us with the past in a deep and fundamental way. And, perhaps most importantly, it's difficult even to hint at the human dimension in work that is too abstract or oblique.

The horror of September 11, 2001, has brought to artists the daunting task of constructing memorials to a new kind of slaughter, even more senseless than war or concentration camps. Plans for new buildings and memorials at the site itself, the former World Trade Center, have been predictably fraught with political and aesthetic controversy. But the many communities in the city and surrounding suburbs that suffered losses in the terrorist attack have also felt the need to honor their dead, and these tributes are now taking shape. In the time-honored manner of such civic projects, competitions are held, artists submit ideas, and commissions are awarded.

Sculptor Sassona Norton answered one such call when Montgomery County, Pennsylvania, advertised for artists to put forward proposals for a memorial that would incorporate a piece of wreckage from the attacks—a bent and twisted I-beam retrieved from the fiery collapse of the North Tower. The concept that won her the contest was disarmingly simple but layered in meaning. A pair of gigantic bronze hands nearly eight feet high cradles the looped and scarred fragment,

itself a weirdly and eerily abstract kind of sculpture. The hands holding the girder are raised on a slanted rectangular shaft atop a circular base 16 feet in diameter, and the base is inscribed with the words:

> *September 11, 2001*
> *The many who died*
> *The many who fought to save others*
> *Memories never die*

The words flow continuously, circling the periphery of the disc. But the separate thoughts have no fixed sequence, and the viewer can start reading the inscription from any point of approach, adding a dynamic of personal experience as well as of perpetual motion.

Norton has worked as a painter for most of her career and is a relative newcomer to sculpture, a medium to which she first turned her full attention in 1999. In that short span of time she has produced an impressive body of work, especially remarkable because she is able to work on both an intimate and a monumental scale. Hands have long been one of her favorite subjects, whether sculpted as objects of interest in and of themselves or combined with expressive heads. She is not the first artist, of course, to realize the emotional potential of hands divorced from the rest of the body. The sixteenth-century German artist Albrecht Dürer produced a drawing of praying hands that has been reproduced ad nauseum on greeting cards and devotional items; French Romantic painter Théodore Géricault painted ghoulishly severed arms, hands, and feet; and the great Auguste Rodin modeled innumerable hands in just about every conceivable "pose." In choosing to show just hands, Norton aligns herself firmly with a modernist tradition in the making since the late nineteenth century. Ever since the radical cropping of figures and scenes that lies at the heart of works by Manet and Degas[1], and continuing through the exercises in fragmentation by Cubist artists, we have no difficulty accepting a part of the body as a metaphor for the whole.

The hands Norton sculpted speak volumes. They are unabashedly masculine. They are also rough — the nails are chipped, the veins are prominent, the skin is weathered and wrinkled. They would seem to belong to someone who might have been at the site soon after the disaster — a fire fighter or policeman or rescue worker. But the way they cradle the girder conveys the utmost delicacy and respect, and in this cautious embrace, the I-beam becomes a flying, slippery shape, almost alive, something that could fly off on its own (or, alternatively, get crushed to death) if not handled carefully.

Norton has said that her first conception for the memorial was for a more horizontal orientation, incorporating a reflecting pool with the hands rising out of the water. When she saw the space of the plaza where the sculpture now stands, and took into account both the architecture of the nineteenth-century Greek Revival courthouse behind it and the demands of a relatively confined area, she modified her initial ideas to show the hands and girder lifted upward. It's a momentous choice, even a life-affirming one. As critic Rosalind Krauss pointed out in an essay on the contemporary photographer Cindy Sherman, "the plane of verticality is the plane of *Prégnanz*, the hanging together or coherence of form . . . . Further, this vertical dimension, in being the axis of form, is also the axis of beauty."[2]

From certain angles, the work also has a dramatic, diagonal Baroque sweep, reminding us of the composition favored by such sculptors as Bernini, who used this kind of upward slanting to convey the desire for flight in works like *Apollo and Daphne*. (More recently, this was the axis used to great effect in the Iwo Jima Monument, which was based on a dramatic photograph of American G.I.s struggling to plant the flag on the first Japanese territory conquered during World War II.)

Norton says that one of her most important decisions in planning the monument involved the position in which the I-beam was to be held. "The torn and twisted metal seemed so organic that no part of it was square or even," she observed in her specifications for the memorial. To create a better sense of balance, she would have to install it at a slight tilt instead of at the conventional 90 degrees, which further suggested the angle of the hands and the supporting shaft. And it is that tilting movement throughout the memorial that engages the viewer and creates the illusion that the girder could shoot off into the sky, even as a slight curve in the metal provides a necessary counterpoint and directs our gaze back toward the outstretched fingers of the right hand.

Like most truly compelling three-dimensional works, Norton's memorial demands to be looked at from different perspectives, and the circular base encourages movement around the sculpture. The meaning for the viewer is left open to interpretation. Norton has spoken of the twisted I-beam as containing a dual symbolism, like that of the Christian cross: "It's an instrument of torture, of horror, turned into a symbol of tenderness, love, and hope," she told a reporter in

2004. The I-beam, in its most functional sense, is also a supposedly sturdy and vital part of building design, one of the elements that holds the architecture together and makes it suitable for human occupation. To see it mangled and charred beyond recognition is to wonder at the force and heat that could reduce it to its present shape, no more steadfast than a bobby pin subjected to high temperatures and bent into a loop. And to see it cradled between a pair of outsized hands has the effect of reducing the girder to human dimensions. This piece of supposedly durable steel is as vulnerable as we are. Lifting it upward conveys a sense of hope and seems to imply that even disaster can be muted and overcome "in the right hands."

But what the work says to the individual who encounters it will ultimately depend on what the viewer brings to it, whether that's a personal loss from the 9/11 atrocities, a love of art history, or a desire for catharsis through the act of looking and reflecting. Its success as a sculpture seems assured; its power as a memorial remains within the hearts and minds of those who need to grieve, remember, or find solace.

[1] Linda Nochlin, *The Body in Pieces: The Fragment as a Metaphor of Modernity* (London: Thames & Hudson, 1994), 25–47.

[2] Rosalind E. Krauss, *Cindy Sherman, 1975–1993*, with an essay by Norman Bryson (New York and London: Rizzoli, 1993), 93–94.

PLATES

9/11 MEMORIAL *Clay version of the sculpture with the I-beam*

9/11 MEMORIAL *The finished sculpture in location*

9/11 MEMORIAL *Detail of the finished sculpture*

9/11 MEMORIAL *The finished sculpture at the unveiling ceremony*

9/11 MEMORIAL *The finished sculpture at the unveiling ceremony*

DEDICATION SPEECH *9/11 Memorial Unveiling Ceremony*

Dear commissioners, distinguished guests, friends and family,

This is a heart-wrenching day. I am filled with two contradictory emotions: deep sadness and pride. Sadness, in the face of the horrific event that brought us to this day, and pride, in giving a voice and a vision to remembering the tragedy on 9/11.

I could not be here today without the help of others. So many have helped to turn the vision I had into the reality in front of you. I am deeply grateful to all of them, and apologize if I don't mention each one by name.

I would like to first thank the commissioners of Montgomery County and their selection committee. They recognized the value of my design and trusted my ability to execute it.

Creating a bronze sculpture of this size requires great teamwork. I could not have sculpted these giant hands without my studio assistants Rob Kellett and Adonis Morris. When you sculpt in clay you have to first build a steel armature for support. Both Rob and Adonis helped to weld it.

Then the hands emerged in clay, and every day I needed to fit them under the I-beam. By the time I completed the sculpting in clay each hand reached 2000 pounds. It took five men to move just one.

I give special thanks for Argos, the foundry in Brewster, New York. Particularly to Roger Erickson, who supervised the entire project, and to Dennis Klubnick who was in charge of the actual metal work. Because of the size, the hands had to be cast in 23 separate parts. Only someone of Dennis' ability could put them back together so seamlessly. And then there was Steve Roy, who applied layers and layers of patina under torch heat to protect the memorial for future generations.

Finally, I want to thank all who expressed interest in this project, particularly the video artist Han Vu who followed the progress with his camera. And last, but not least, I am grateful to Reed, my husband to be, for his support. It was not easy living with me for the last year and a half.

Today, I wanted to share with you some thoughts and feelings that have occupied me since I started to work on the memorial.

First and foremost, my heart goes out to any and all who have lost loved ones in the 9/11 attack. No memorial can express the pain—so private and individual—the suffering, and the tragic change of life that you have gone through—and still might.

When I first heard about 9/11, I was in my studio in London. But my sister had just been to New York to visit and went, naturally, to the World Trade Center. She left to go back home just a few days before 9/11. It still makes me think—and quite often—about the randomness in which some of us were personally spared, while others were not. Yet, we all were impacted. Life as we had known it has changed. Collectively.

It is to this collective experience that I tried to give a voice.

When the commissioners of Montgomery County announced the competition to design and build the 9/11 memorial, they stipulated that it would have to include an I-beam that was once a part of the North Tower of the World Trade Center.

I welcomed the idea full-heartedly, as an American and as an artist.

The I-beam is a witness to the tragedy. It is also its victim as well as its symbol. Like the towers, the I-beam became an unwilling participant in the horrors of the day.

Look at it: It was torn, folded on itself twice, completely twisted. From an everyday element of construction, industrial in character, it turned into something mystical. From a cold and man-made form it turned into an organic shape. I saw this change as evidence of the destruction, but I also wanted to use it as an opportunity to express transformation and hope.

I have never had a relationship with an inanimate object similar to what I have developed with the I-beam. I first saw it on my trip to Norristown when I was notified that I was among the finalists. I was taken to the fire fighters academy where it had been lying on the floor for quite some time, and from the first minute I saw it, I felt as if it were alive. I got down on my knees and touched it.

The I-beam lived in front of my studio for long months; I removed the studio doors, but it was still too large to be moved in, so it hung outside, suspended on cables from a temporary 20-foot-tall structure. Every day, at 7 o'clock in the morning, I would walk to my studio through the woods. But Rob, my assistant, was always there earlier, and he would raise the I-beam that had been lowered to the ground the night before. From the distance, through the woods, I could hear the sound of the I-beam being pulled up against the cables, link by link. The sound was rhythmic, and melodious, and very peaceful. Just like bells. And it would fill my heart with tenderness.

To express tenderness as well as hope, the I-beam is lifted upward into the sky by a large pair of hands. The hands cradle the I-beam, but their sheer size reflects strength, as well as tenderness.

What happened on 9/11 included so many acts of heroism and sacrifice that it is not difficult to imagine the lifting of the I-beam also as an expression of resilience and courage.

So many were involved in acts of bravery in response to the urgent call for help. The first responders: from the fire fighters to the police officers to the medics—everyone who was around in one way or another—all fought to lift, and to save lives. I wanted to create the image of lifting as we might envision it in a moment of duress: a large pair of hands that can reach out to us. The hands are strong, muscular, and experienced. They have known time. They have known life. And they are capable of rising above everything to carry us from wherever we are—into safety.

Consequent acts since 9/11 engage expressions of lifting as well. What took place on that day: the lifting of fallen particles and debris in order to uncover and carry the victims out into daylight—has changed later into construction. The broken parts are lifted now in order to clear the site for a future rebuilt.

I hope that the acts of lifting that were the core image of the memorial hold a promise for some solace. I hope that remembering 9/11, remembering the many who were killed so randomly, and remembering the first responders who fought to save others—may bring some peace. I hope that pain—as unwanted and as unwarranted—holds some lessons that we may discover in the process.

Reflecting on the past can make us collectively stronger. Including the past in our thoughts for a better future can make us collectively whole.

Memories never die.

If any of this reaches some spot in the heart of a viewer—I would feel rewarded.

Thank you.

Sassona Norton

September 8, 2005
Norristown, Pennsylvania

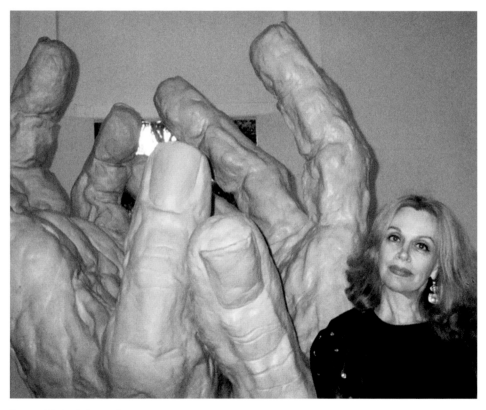

Sassona Norton in her studio

ACKNOWLEDGMENTS

To Steven Miller, executive director of the Morris Museum, for his creative force and vision that initiated this show and turned it into a reality. In placing the sculptures together, Steven has elevated them from their singularity and gave them a collective voice.

To Mary Chandor, chairperson of the Board of Trustees, and to all the members of the Board for their vote of confidence and constant support.

To the museum staff, and particularly to Laura Galvanek, Erin Dougherty, Kim Tauriello, and Betty Heinig for their untiring efforts and skills in executing the daily tasks of organizing the show.

To Argos Foundry for the multi phase reproduction of my work. The success of the final sculptures could not have been achieved without the efforts of the many wax, metal, and patina technicians to execute every detail of the creative process.

To Robert Kellett and Adonis Morris, my studio assistants, whose dedicated help has enabled me to reach for larger scale and greater impact.

To art critics Ann Landi and Hilarie Sheets for their insightful essays. In their individual eloquence they have captured and given voice to my artistic essence.

To George Erml, Han Vu, and Scott Whittle, who succeeded in the difficult task of transferring the three dimensions of my sculpture into the two dimensions of photography.

To David Chickey of Skolkin+Chickey for this beautiful and elegant book. Without his extraordinary eye, none of it could have happened.

First Edition

2006 © Morris Museum

6 Normandy Heights Road

Morristown, NJ 07960

www.morrismuseum.org

ISBN 1 886193 06 1

Design: David Chickey / Skolkin+Chickey

Editor: Catherine Fleming

Proofreader: Laura Addison

Photography: George Erml, Han Vu, Scott Whittle, and Bruce White

Color separations: Wes Pittman

Printed and bound by Tien Wah Press, Singapore

Library of Congress Cataloging-in-Publication Data available upon request.

frontispiece: *An Hour Before Dawn*, 2001, PLATE 2
page 4: *First Rain*, 2002, PLATE 6
page 6: *To Whom Do I Pray*, 2005, PLATE 15